Reflect

Spiritual Wisdom

"If God is for us, who can be against us?"
Romans 8:31

Alisa D. Deeds

Spiritual Wisdom
Trilogy Christian Publishers, a Wholly Owned Subsidiary of the Trinity Broadcasting Network
2442 Michelle Drive, Tustin, CA 92780
Copyright © 2023 by Alisa D. Deeds
Unless otherwise indicated, scripture quotations are taken from The Daily Walk Bible, NIV. Hoover, J.W., Kirk, P.A., and Tiegreen, C. (2013) The Daily Walk Bible. Explore God's Path to Life. Tyndale House Publishers, Inc. Carol Stream, IL. Scripture quotations marked NIV are taken from the Holy Bible, New International Version®, NIV®. Copyright © 1973, 1978, 1984, 2011 by Biblica, Inc.TM Used by permission of Zondervan. All rights reserved worldwide. www.zondervan.com. The "NIV" and "New International Version" are trademarks registered in the United States Patent and Trademark Office by Biblica, Inc.TM

No part of this book may be reproduced, stored in a retrieval system, or transmitted by any means without written permission from the author. All rights reserved. Printed in the USA.
Rights Department, 2442 Michelle Drive, Tustin, CA 92780.
Trilogy Christian Publishing/TBN and colophon are trademarks of Trinity Broadcasting Network.
For information about special discounts for bulk purchases, please contact Trilogy Christian Publishing.
Trilogy Disclaimer: The views and content expressed in this book are those of the author and may not necessarily reflect the views and doctrine of Trilogy Christian Publishing or the Trinity Broadcasting Network.
Manufactured in the United States of America
10 9 8 7 6 5 4 3 2 1
Library of Congress Cataloging-in-Publication Data is available.
ISBN: 979-8-88738-237-1
E-ISBN: 979-8-88738-238-8

All scripture is from:

The Daily Walk Bible, NIV.

Hoover, J.W., Kirk, P.A., and Tiegreen, C. (2013) The Daily Walk Bible. Explore God's Path to Life. Tyndale House Publishers, Inc. Carol Stream, IL.

For Adam and Jake

Spiritual Wisdom

"God is within her,
she will not fall."
Psalm 46:5

SCRIPTURE

Spiritual Wisdom

Don't comfort what you should confront.

WISDOM

Spiritual Wisdom

A grateful heart protects you from negative thinking.

TRUTH

Spiritual Wisdom

Your heredity is not your destiny.

BELIEVE

Spiritual Wisdom

"Those who look to him are radiant; their faces are never covered with shame."
Psalm 34:5

SCRIPTURE

Spiritual Wisdom

God will not change our circumstances until He first changes us.

CONSIDER

Spiritual Wisdom

You have not, because you ask not.

TRUTH

Spiritual Wisdom

I have a strong, sound mind—weakness is for the enemy.

WISDOM

Spiritual Wisdom

"Weeping may stay for the night, but rejoicing comes in the morning."
Psalm 30:5

SCRIPTURE

Spiritual Wisdom

There is happiness for those who trust in the Lord.

BELIEVE

Spiritual Wisdom

God: not my will, but Yours. Thank You that You are giving me strength.

GRACE

Spiritual Wisdom

Don't worry, and don't fret;
just trust God.

WISDOM

Spiritual Wisdom

"Be kind and compassionate to one another, forgiving each other, just as in Christ God forgave you."
Ephesians 4:32

SCRIPTURE

Spiritual Wisdom

God being for you is more than the world being against you.

IMAGINE

Spiritual Wisdom

You will stop needing approval from others when you learn to approve of yourself.

BELIEVE

Spiritual Wisdom

Stop focusing on the circumstances that can't be changed and focus on those that can.

BE THANKFUL

Spiritual Wisdom

"I will extol the Lord at all times; his praise will always be on my lips."
Psalm 34:1

SCRIPTURE

Spiritual Wisdom

Don't aim to be happy all the time, but aim to love yourself all the time.

APPRECIATION

Spiritual Wisdom

It is not about you.
It is not about me.
It is about God.

TRUTH

Spiritual Wisdom

Not everyone can function without applause; can you escape the noise of the crowd?

CONSIDER

Spiritual Wisdom

"Anxiety weighs down the heart, but a kind word cheers it up."
Proverbs 12:25

SCRIPTURE

Spiritual Wisdom

Knowledge = Empowerment

WISDOM

Spiritual Wisdom

Give a man a mask, and he will reveal his true self.

TRUTH

Spiritual Wisdom

What is over your head is under His feet.

GRACE

Spiritual Wisdom

"Your word is a lamp for my feet, a light on my path."
Psalm 119:105

SCRIPTURE

Spiritual Wisdom

Just for today,
be kind to yourself.

WISDOM

Spiritual Wisdom

Dwell in the possibility.

BELIEVE

Spiritual Wisdom

Be all that you are and nothing that you are not.

TRUTH

Spiritual Wisdom

"Resentment kills a fool,
and envy slays the simple."
Job 5:2

SCRIPTURE

Spiritual Wisdom

God can dream bigger dreams than you can dream for yourself.

BELIEVE

Spiritual Wisdom

The greatest witness is your walk.

KNOWLEDGE

Spiritual Wisdom

Think about what you are thinking about.

CONSIDER

Spiritual Wisdom

"Pride goes before destruction, a haughty spirit before a fall."
Proverbs 16:18

SCRIPTURE

Spiritual Wisdom

Negative thoughts equal negative feelings.

WISDOM

Spiritual Wisdom

Patience is a necessity, not a preference.

TRUTH

Spiritual Wisdom

There was never a night that could defeat the sunrise.

BELIEVE

Spiritual Wisdom

"Vindicate me in your righteousness, Lord my God; do not let them gloat over me."
Psalm 35:24

SCRIPTURE

Spiritual Wisdom

Life is always a risk,
never a possession.

BE GRATEFUL

Spiritual Wisdom

Brokenness is God's requirement for maximum usefulness.

GRACE

Spiritual Wisdom

Panic, not the task, is the enemy.

KNOWLEDGE

Spiritual Wisdom

"Better a dry crust with peace and quiet than a house full of feasting, with strife."
Proverbs 17:1

SCRIPTURE

Spiritual Wisdom

God makes all things work for good, but that doesn't mean it always feels good.

BELIEVE

Spiritual Wisdom

Hold tightly to what God has put in your heart, but hold loosely to how it's going to happen.

KNOWLEDGE

Spiritual Wisdom

God is working out His plan for your life.

BELIEVE

Spiritual Wisdom

"Freely you have received;
freely give."
Matthew 10:8

SCRIPTURE

Spiritual Wisdom

The best way to get love is to give it.

WISDOM

Spiritual Wisdom

God will reveal things in accordance with His will.

BELIEVE

Spiritual Wisdom

Lean not on your own understanding.

GRACE

Spiritual Wisdom

"Do not let your hearts be troubled. You believe in God; believe also in me."
John 14:1

SCRIPTURE

Spiritual Wisdom

If you want things to change, you must change.
If you want things to get better, you must get better.

TRUTH

Spiritual Wisdom

God always ignores your present level of completeness in favor of your ultimate future completeness.

KNOWLEDGE

Spiritual Wisdom

You cannot take a day off spiritually and remain spiritual.

WISDOM

Spiritual Wisdom

"For God is not a God of disorder but of peace."
1 Corinthians 14:33

SCRIPTURE

Spiritual Wisdom

Do you want to feel the pain of discipline, or the pain of regret?

APPRECIATION

Spiritual Wisdom

Worry ends when faith begins.

TRUST

Spiritual Wisdom

"You no more need a holiday from spiritual concentration than your heart needs a holiday from beating."
Oswald Chambers

WISDOM

Spiritual Wisdom

"Walk with the wise and become wise, for a companion of fools suffers harm."

Proverbs 13:20

SCRIPTURE

Spiritual Wisdom

Do not go through—grow through; learn from it. You are learning and growing on the inside.

KNOWLEDGE

Spiritual Wisdom

"In a dark time, the eye begins to see."
Theodore Roethke

BELIEVE

Spiritual Wisdom

There is nothing more powerful than a changed mind.

WISDOM

Spiritual Wisdom

"I have been crucified with Christ and I no longer live, but Christ lives in me."
Galatians 2:20

SCRIPTURE

Spiritual Wisdom

You do not get results without rituals.

INSPIRATION

Spiritual Wisdom

It is not the things, but what one thinks of the things, that counts.

BE GRATEFUL

Spiritual Wisdom

Do not *decide* to accept any limitations today

BELIEVE

Spiritual Wisdom

"Starting a quarrel is like breaching a dam; so drop the matter before a dispute breaks out."
Proverbs 17:14

SCRIPTURE

Spiritual Wisdom

"The part can never be well unless the whole is well."
Plato

WISDOM

Spiritual Wisdom

Control your mind—don't let it control you.

KNOWLEDGE

Spiritual Wisdom

There is purpose and meaning in today; do not rush through it.

BE GRATEFUL

Spiritual Wisdom

"For you know the grace of our Lord Jesus Christ, that though he was rich, yet for your sake he became poor, so that you through his poverty might become rich."
2 Corinthians 8:9

SCRIPTURE

Spiritual Wisdom

What you are unwilling to walk away from is where you will always stay stuck.

TRUTH

Spiritual Wisdom

There will always be someone who does not like you; move on.

KNOWLEDGE

Spiritual Wisdom

Do not let other people incite you to unrest.

TRUTH

Spiritual Wisdom

"Have I not commanded you? Be strong and courageous. Do not be afraid; do not be discouraged, for the Lord your God will be with you wherever you go."
Joshua 1:9

SCRIPTURE

Spiritual Wisdom

Grateful people focus on the positive. They are grateful to be alive.

BE GRATEFUL

Spiritual Wisdom

"Remember who you are— you are not some special being created in heaven, but a sinner saved by grace."
Oswald Chambers

WISDOM

Spiritual Wisdom

Progress, not perfection, because perfection is not possible.

APPRECIATION

Spiritual Wisdom

"You judge by human standards; I pass judgement on no one."
John 8:15

SCRIPTURE

Spiritual Wisdom

Rejoice as you journey with Jesus together toward heaven.

BELIEVE

Spiritual Wisdom

God spoke the world into existence; His power is unlimited.

GRACE

Spiritual Wisdom

Instead of trying to fight your fears, concentrate on trusting Jesus. Human weakness, consecrated to God, draws His strength into you.

BELIEVE

Spiritual Wisdom

"Jesus answered, 'I am the way and the truth and the life. No one comes to the Father except through me.'"
John 14:6

SCRIPTURE

Spiritual Wisdom

Those who do not reflect, project.

TRUTH

Spiritual Wisdom

You are not your thoughts;
you are what you do.

KNOWLEDGE

Spiritual Wisdom

Do the right thing when it is hard.

WISDOM

Spiritual Wisdom

"The Lord searches every heart and understands every desire and every thought."
1 Chronicles 28:9

SCRIPTURE

Spiritual Wisdom

Some trials in life are tests, so God can see how much He can trust us with.

BE THANKFUL

Spiritual Wisdom

Some saints cannot do menial work while maintaining a saintly attitude, because they feel such service is beneath their dignity.

TRUTH

Spiritual Wisdom

God is not separating you to show you what a wonderful person He could make of you, but to reveal His Son in you.

GRACE

Spiritual Wisdom

"And now these three remain: faith, hope and love. But the greatest of these is love."

1 Corinthians 13:13

SCRIPTURE

Spiritual Wisdom

You are free to choose the path you will take, but you are not free to escape the consequences of your choices.

KNOWLEDGE

Spiritual Wisdom

You don't need to be perfect—just consistent.

WISDOM

Spiritual Wisdom

Walk by faith, not by sight.

TRUST

Spiritual Wisdom

"Put on the full armor of God, so that you can take your stand against the devil's schemes."
Ephesians 6:11

SCRIPTURE

Spiritual Wisdom

He chose you before you chose Him.

BELIEVE

Spiritual Wisdom

Your limited mindset comes from the enemy.

TRUTH

Spiritual Wisdom

God's ways are not our ways—get in agreement with God.

KNOWLEDGE

Spiritual Wisdom

"Forget the former things;
do not dwell on the past."
Isaiah 43:18

SCRIPTURE

Spiritual Wisdom

God does not define us by our mistakes; He refines us by our mistakes.

GRACE

Spiritual Wisdom

Accept yourself just as you are; you don't need to prove yourself to anyone.

WISDOM

Spiritual Wisdom

Are you using where you are today as an explanation, or an excuse?

TRUTH

Spiritual Wisdom

"You are my God, and I will praise you; you are my God, and I will exalt you."
Psalm 118:28

SCRIPTURE

Printed in the USA
CPSIA information can be obtained
at www.ICGtesting.com
LVHW010941110923
757503LV00005B/65